MANNA:
HALLELUIAH TO THE
LAMB OF GOD!

MANNA:
HALLELUIAH TO THE LAMB OF GOD!

PART 8

JUDITH WILLIAMS

MANNA: HALLELUIAH TO THE LAMB OF GOD!
PART 8

21st Century King James Version (KJ21)
Copyright © 1994 by Deuel Enterprises, Inc.

Blue Red and Gold Letter Edition™
Copyright © 2012 BRG Bible Ministries.
Used by Permission. All rights reserved.

iUniverse books may be ordered through booksellers or by contacting:

iUniverse
1663 Liberty Drive
Bloomington, IN 47403
www.iuniverse.com
844-349-9409

ISBN: 978-1-6632-1884-1 (sc)
ISBN: 978-1-6632-1885-8 (e)

Print information available on the last page.

iUniverse rev. date: 07/30/2021

CONTENTS

INTRODUCTION

Happy New Year 2021! I woke up at 3:46 am this morning to pen a few lines for this 8th volume. It's January, which derives its name from the Latin Januarius (see Janus), the Roman god who presided over doors and beginnings. Indeed, we will experience new and exciting openings in 2021 as doors open for the First-fruits and the remnant of God. It will nonetheless close on the class that is found to be unfaithful.

It's a new day as we are carried over the threshold into a new realm.

Jeremiah 33:6 *"Behold I will bring it health and cure, and I will cure them, and I will reveal unto them the abundance of peace and truth."*

God promises to restore us and make us whole again.

The world has changed so dramatically in recent years that it has become confusing with all these unprecedented crises occurring one after the other.

God knows that man of himself cannot find his way in this dark world as says in his blended thoughts:

Jeremiah 10:23 *"O Lord, I know that the way of man is not in himself: it is not in man that walketh to direct his steps."*

Hosea 12:13 *"Therefore God sends prophets to guide the people and help them to make right choices for God's people are led by a prophet and are preserved by a prophet."*

What a gloomy world we would live in if we had no way of knowing our past or of knowing the future! But while we may have knowledge of our past and of our future, it is the present that gives us the most comfort in knowing. Hence current events must be interpreted in the right light so we can move safely.

By god's grace I have been blessed with information that can lighten our path as we head home. If I were to use my human wisdom all I could produce was something fit for the dumpster! But this is God's theory not man's. You see, God is not experimenting as He is omniscient, omnipotent and omnipresent. Herein this little book will be revealed the beauty and symmetry of the truth – the Gospel truth.

It will reveal the mystery of godliness and the mystery of iniquity. We have been given the keys of the Kingdom Church, and we have the codes to unlock the prophecies that are now unsealed. Amen.

CHAPTER ONE

GOD'S ABIDING PRESENCE WITH US: THE BIDEN STORY

So, God remembered His promise to Father Abraham to give His seed the land of Palestine, there to establish themselves as a kingdom of saints. Therefore, in 1963, He sent Neilia Hunter to Nassau, Bahamas on a Spring Break. There she met Joe Biden who was also on Spring Break from Syracuse University where he was a junior.

Why Bahamas? Bahamas is symbolic of the Babylonian system. There on Nassau, and the 700 islands and cays is nestled the headquarters and main capital of Babylon. On the Abaco islands is a national state park named Tilloo, which serves as a 'till' for the god of mammon and the 'loo' an English 'throne'

Green Turtle Bay Park is another symbol of Babylon as this park is a symbol of the mystery woman in Revelation 12 who has a golden cup in her hand. This cup however is a green turtle cup named "Dick's Last Resort" that smells green with all the 'filthiness of her fornication' and her abominable practices spilling all over the place.

The Lord must put an end to this system and usher in a period of righteousness.

The name Neilia is a Hebrew name meaning "locking, closing". In the end time, the closing work for the church is the sealing of the 144, 000. (Revelation 14:1-5). When this work is complete the sealed ones are locked inside the Banquet Hall, while the unbelieving ones without the seal are locked out forever. (Matthew 25)

Neilia Hunter and Joe Biden went on to get married in 1966 and the union went on to produce three children. God had in His great plan decreed that the middle son, Hunter Biden would be used to fulfil the prophecy on Genesis 3:15.

Genesis 3:15 *"And I will put enmity between thee and the woman, and between thy seed and her seed; it shall bruise thy head and thou shalt bruise his heel."*

This means that sin had to be hunted and destroyed. The bruising that the serpent receives renders him incapable of action – he becomes disabled.

Although the enemy tried to wipe out the family on a December afternoon, the Biden boys were spared. However, Mom and daughter died in a car accident. So fifty-six years after his mom died, in 2019 an investigation of Hunter Biden in Ukraine led to the impeachment of the 45th president of the United States, Donald Trump, who began to look for 'dirt' on the family, especially Joe Biden, his political rival.

The impeachment dealt a deathblow to his presidency and he went on to lose the General elections in 2020 after only a term in office.

Hunter's grandfather, Joe Robinette Sr. from Scranton, PA was a decent, hardworking man. The light would shine from his offspring as his hometown is nicknamed "The Electric City." No wonder Donald Trump says the junior Biden was not born in the Electric City. He obviously has deep fear of the light! The light would surely destroy him.

The Kingdom is Unfolding

2001 September 11	The Twin Towers collapsed in bomb blast in New York City
	Clearing the way.
2002	My journey to Nassau, Bahamas for teaching post at Queen's College
2003	Returned home The Old Man on the mountain collapsed in New Hampshire. The works of man and their pomp and pride will be laid low
2005	Katrina storm devastated New Orleans. Light made landfall. K@t – reena Tares separated from wheat in figure
2007	Handel graduates High School. Craig turns 20. We travelled to the State of Oregon.
2008	Michael Strachan N.F.L. Giant quarterback wins Super Bowl with these words: "Stomp you out!" Giants – 17 PATS – 14 The mustard seed of truth had grown into a giant tree. Mark 4:30; Luke 13: 18, 19; Matthew 13:31, 32
	Paving the Way
	Barack Obama elected 1st African American (Black) president of the United States of America.
2011	Kate Middleton married Prince William of England which is a type of the first temple restored. Back in the middle!
2015	Pope Francis visited Republicans in Congress to initiate the letting loose of the four winds of Revelation 7.

The bishops of Rome can read dark sentences. They do so by the supernatural aid of agents from the spiritual underworld. They all know what is to be. When Pope Francis the Republican-led Congress, John "the bane of our lives" Boehner, resigned as Speaker of the House and Paul Ryan took over.

Ryan hails from the State of Wisconsin which ends in "sin" and has con in the middle. The man of sin had come to discharge the Mark of the Beast endgame. The system will turn on the remnant for refusing to bow down to the beast and its image once all this is set in motion. According to Gordon Sondlin, former ambassador to the European Union, "It's a drug (done) deal."

The $600.00 Covid-19 relief stimulus from the Government is a symbol of the restoration of the Kingdom during the 6th seal of Revelation it carries the sign of the Kingdom restored. Trump wants to offer $1400.00 which is a backway offer from Babylon the Great. Newt Gringrich agrees with Trump and wants 80% of Americans to get what they want, and deserve.

That 80% is really statement to establish an earth wide dominion in a sin-infested domain.
(8 x 10) = 80

Gringrich's wife Callista is the current ambassador to the Vatican and they have a "list" of all who will turn from man and worship the true God to persecute them.

2016	Donald Trump is elected as the 45th president of the United States
2018	Wrote manuscript, ***Manna: A Consecrated G.P.S. Guide into the Promised Land***
2019	President Trump impeached by the House of Representatives.
2020	Manna volume 1 released February 14. Covid-19 pandemic ensues. Trump loses General elections. Biden & Kamala ticket won.

God promises to set up His Eternal Kingdom during the reign of the 45th President. Trump is to be the last of the Beast-powers to rule over God's people (Daniel 2:44-45).
Hence, Barack Obama's presidency marked the initial phase of the Kingdom of glory. (Psalm 44).

God, then suspended operations to do "House Cleaning" at the White House to make it "pure and clean."

"Here's your Mouse!"
(Psalm 45)
After the presidency of Trump collapses into the dust, it's time for Joe Biden to be restored as a true servant to Build * Back * Better.

(Psalm 46)
Neilia's desires and wishes have come true!

Indeed, the promises of God are sure and we can rely on them to be fulfilled wholeheartedly. Hunter's brother, Beau, had the spirit of the living creatures in him as he served humanity in Kosova in dedicated style. The curse on mankind is broken and the "eggs" (ova) of sin are destroyed.

Ezekiel 1:28
"As the appearance of the bow (Beau) that is in the cloud in the day of rain, (U-Kraine) so was the likeness of the Lord." Beau departed this life at age 46, the very position his father now holds as the 46th president of the United States of America. It's a new day. Neilia won again!

CHAPTER TWO

THE UNITED STATES: LAMB-LIKE BEAST SPEAKS AS A DRAGON

America in prophecy is found in Revelation 13:11 where a beast comes up out of the earth with lamb-like horns yet spake as a dragon.

Revelation 13:11 *"And I beheld another beast coming up out of the earth; and he had two horns like a lamb, and he spake as a dragon."*

The United States of America has been most blessed of all nations by the Most High God. Here in this nation has God established the Headquarters of His living church.

The U.S. Flag

The **red** bars on the US flag symbolizes sin and bloodshed. Many nations on earth have red colour on their flags symbolizing the world in a sin-convulsed state.

The **white** backdrop symbolizes sorrow and surrender and those who make no sacrifice on the altar of contrition. They "shed no blood" to gain the cross as they take the easy, smooth path to destruction that ends in eternal sorrows.

The **blue** square on the right of the flag with the 50-state stars is a symbol of depression and the stars are a a representation of the satanic hosts that were drawn by the dragon's tail from heaven to earth. Hence our battle is not only with flesh and blood.

Ephesians 6:12 *"For we wrestle not against flesh and blood, but against principalities, against powers, against the rulers of the darkness of this world, against spiritual wickedness in high places."*

Revelation 12:4 *"And his tail drew the third part of the stars of heaven, and did cast them to the earth."*

The U.S. National Anthem

The Star Spangled Banner is a tribute to the idol Baal. The '*Oh*' is really '*Ho*' in reverse and '*see*' has reference to the Holy See (Vatican) and God's hiding place in Tenne*see*. The images of '*rockets' red glare*', '*the bombs bursting in air*' are suggestive of war which the devil loves for it stirs up worst passions in the heart, and creates havoc in its wake. What is '*half conceals*', '*half discloses*' if not an attempt to deceive even the very elect? See **Matthew 24:24**. That's how hell operates – by grand deception.

> *"Their blood has washed out their foul footsteps' pollution. No refuge could save the hireling and slave from the terror of flight, or the gloom of the grave."*

These morbid images speak of Satan's desire to keep men in bondage of death and the grave forever! Colin Kaepernick (N.F.L. star) resisted this supremacy.

July 4th Independence Day

July 4th is not a date for freedom.

It is a date honoring Hagar's House of Bondage and Satan's vast lazar house.

The number 4 relates to the worshippers of the sun gods as deities who help and sustain them.

Sarah, Abraham's wife, left idolatry and worshipped the true God. Hagar was a bondwoman, bound in chains of sin. So she rightly represents those who worship idols.

The number 4 also references the four day's journey Christ took to Lazarus' tomb. It took Him 4 days to illustrate that mankind was trapped in a vast lazar house because they worshipped the wrong sun and not the **Sun of Righteousness.**

So, July 4th is really a holiday to worship the sun god Baal which is a form of idolatry!

The Bald Eagle vs The Golden Eagle

Babylon is described as a '**habitation of devils, and the hold of every foul spirit, and a cage of every unclean and hateful bird**' Revelation 18:2.

Hair is a symbol of glory and men with beards and women with long hair are 'glorified'. The choice of the bald eagle as a national symbol states that the US has been changed into Babylon.

We can see that coming to light when Derrick "FoxyCrow and Friends" Chauvin knelt in George Floyd's neck and took his life. The surname Chauvin means 'BALD' (hateful bird)

The Golden Eagle is Mexico's official symbol and the eagle appears on its flag.

Proudly we Hail

Pride is never good.

Proverbs 16:18 (KJV) *"Pride goeth before destruction, and a haughty spirit before a fall."*

The self-sufficient one will slip and slide every which way like the Proud Boys who were called on to "stand down" (downward slide).

The Alabama Flag

The Alabama flag shall be a crimson cross of St. Andrew on a field of white.

The Alabama flag therefore is a configuration of the US flag with the emblems of Satanic stars removed. This flag predicts the overthrow of the kingdom of darkness.

In 2017, at the College Football game between Georgia and Alabama, the enemy was told in the score that his end was near. President Trump and Vice-President Pence attended the game and the score was

Georgia 23   **Alabama** 26

Total 49

This judgment score was fulfilled when the Abaco 'floods' caused by Dorian hurricane came to Alabama in Sharpie-gate and got swallowed up. Yes, Alabama opened her mouth and swallowed up the devil's flood fulfilling Revelation 12. The earth is now sweet and light.

The Alabama flag got further configuration when the star emblem was removed and in the right corner of the flag now stands a square depicting an Orange tree by the sea. The square now depicts HALLELUJAH SQUARE!

Alabama's anthem is a song of triumph of the redeemed. Satanic hosts viewed the purified and got angry. Then they conspired to let loose the winds of strife to wipe out civilization but they were already defeated.

The State Song

Alabama, Alabama
We will aye be true to thee
From thy southern shore where growth,
By the sea thine orange tree...

Godlier than the land that Moses
Climbed lone Nebo's Mount to see
Alabama. Alabama
We will aye be true to thee.

The Jamaican Flag

The Jamaican flag colors depict the sacrificial ceremonial system built in the tabernacle of Moses. It is a flag that represents the sacrificial attitude of its people who blend with heaven to help save suffering humanity.

On one level the color **green** symbolizes our green vegetation, the **gold/ yellow** the sunshine and the **black** our struggles as a people.

In the tabernacle the green represents the green shittim wood overlaid with gold (yellow). The black represents the black skins. (Exodus 35-38).

The Kingdom Flag

In the flag's backdrop of **green** symbolizing green pastures lies a white circle of rays. The white signifies purity and light. The twelve **blue** stars are a symbol of God's government (Isaiah 52, Revelation 12) here on earth. The lion emblem is the Lion of the Tribe of Judah who breaks every chain.

Answerer Book 4 page 26 *"To Present-truth believers, one of the surest evidences that the Lord is leading in the work of Mt. Carmel, is that regardless of ceaseless opposition, paucity of laborers, and many other handicaps, the work is steadily moving onward with an irresistible power. It is indeed like the mustard seed."*

Answerer Book 4 page 96, 97 *"Despite its humble, insignificant beginning, the criticism and the opposition against it, and the multiform obstacles and impediments which it has had to surmount, it is awakening multitudes throughout Laodicea. It has launch the ship of Reformation and while many have already boarded it, others are rapidly approaching the decision to seek the safety it affords. They are restudying the Bible in the Divine light of the Shepherd's Rod. The Three Angels' Messages have become to them as clear and sweet as a mountain stream. And those who never believed, the writings of the Spirit of Prophecy, are now purchasing all the volumes."*

The Assyrian Yoke

Having been scattered from our beloved homeland we have had to contend with various repressive governments. God's people are held in communist regimes and regimes that enslave people. God is about to change that. Says He:

Isaiah 14:25 *"That I will break the Assyrian in my land, and upon my mountains tread them under foot: then shall his yoke depart from off them, and his burden depart from off their shoulders."*

An oppressive system is built into this landscape. The International Monetary Fund (I.M.F.) is really a code for "I'm a Mother F***er That is why JFK Airport (named after the 35th president of the US) in Queens, New York is the code for John, Mother F***er Airport.

On January 1, 2021 a couple from Queens who work at LSU Café at JFK were killed in a hit and drive crash in New York.

IRS for Internal Revenue Service is the domestic tax collecting bureau. It is the code for: I'ma Raterpillar Snake!

CHAPTER THREE

THE CHRISTMAS MYTH: SANTA CLAUS AND MR. FROST·BITE

Christmas Day, December 25, is widely celebrated as the birthday of Jesus. For starters, Christ Jesus was born on the 3rd of April AD in the spring.

Colors of Christmas

Santa's red and white outfit is a symbol of sin and bloodshed; with the white meaning sorrow. His "black-belt" belies his jolly demeanor for he loves violence. The green color represents immature fruits and those who are not ripened for the heavenly garner. That is why we have the Green Grinch!

"Ho, Ho, Ho"

Santa says 'ho, ho, ho' because it's a call glorifying homosexuality. He carries a sack on his back which is really his scrotum. The 12 days of Christmas carol glorifies the Lesbian movement on the 9th day with "9 ladies dancing". Then why would you have "6 geese-a-laying" when there are beautiful, majestic birds such as peacocks?

Babylon's "gold ring" has reference to the "anus" and the 10 lords-a-leaping can only be the unclean spirits like frogs leaping about. (see Revelation 16:13)

The "8 maids-a-milking" is symbolic of the milkmaid and her pail which stifles dreams and expectations.

The Chimney

Santa comes down the chimney yet the heat does not cause him to fly or rise up as he uses a sleigh to get around. The chimney then is the **Big Tobacco Industry** that encourages smoking. Smoking is a filthy habit that defiles the temple of God. We must not use our nostrils as chimneys.

Reindeer Sleigh

The choice of animal to travel is used because the reindeer has plenty horns that symbolize political power (domination). The sleigh with a "T" at the end becomes "sleight of hand" which makes Santa a big gambler. Yes, the casinos and state lotteries are designed to make the rich richer and the poor poorer yet.

The reindeer carries a lot of "rain water" which is a euphemism for liquor. December is the time for hedonistic pleasures and to get "under your waters". So, the liquor industry is designed to poison and make addicts of the human race. Remember Rayshard Brooks who died at the hands of the police in Georgia? He was "under his waters" when he was shot in the back and died.

Titles of Santa

1. Father Christmas
   John 8:44 *"Ye are of your father the devil, and the lust of your father ye will do..."*

2. Good Saint Nick
   Revelation 2:6 *"But this thou hast, that thou hatest the deeds of the Nicolaitans which I also hate."*

3. Father Frost
   The frosty snowman is a symbol of the cold winter of sin that bites.

The Practice of Tree Cutting

Jeremiah 10:2,3 "Thus saith the Lord, Learn not the way of the heathen, and be not dismayed at the signs of heaven; for the heathen are dismayed at them. For the custom of the people are vain: for one cutteth a tree out of the forest, the work of the hands of the of the workman, with the axe."

If cutting down a tree removes it from the source of life, how can that symbol be used to celebrate birth and life? Seems like Santa has a death wish for you!

Why the 25th Day
2 – fold error (dung)
5 – fold error (5 senses)
Satan appeals to us through our senses.

Rudolf the Red Nose Reindeer and Eric

The "red nose" of Rudolf that shines at night represents the Tabloid Industry with their noses in people's business.

Proverbs 11:13 *"A talebearer revealeth secrets; but he that is of a faithful spirit concealeth the matter"*

The practice of reporting and rebroadcasting of sensitive private matters is offensive to God.

One area of intrusion also relates to the Pro-Life Movement. What is your nose doing in people's business under the guise of love for the unborn? Eric Rudolf an activist for the unborn set off a bomb at Centennial Park in Atlanta to protest abortions. The coward then ran for his life when hunted down. He damaged Emily Lyon's face in an attack on a clinic in Roswell, Georgia. She survived and continues her work.

Before Eric was finally apprehended he was at a Save Right Dumpster foraging for food! So, the Centennial Olympic Park bomber is serving life imprisonment without parole. What a waste!

I cannot for the life of me understand why such a delightful activity in the "bed of the undefiled" must become so hideous in the daylight! The justices who preside over these discussions (Row-Roe vs. Wade) should be privy to other details so we can know if the male extended his full "six-inches". Hmmmm. How deep and how wide was it? How many rotations per minute must be made so as not to incur infractions? Would one risk imprisonment if done in a "fast and furious" fashion? Slow and easy, perhaps? How comes the men get away scotch-free and the women suffer the "ill consequences"? God has given us reason and we must use it.

The real crime here is bringing a child into the world to suffer neglect and abuse because of inadequate care. A child in the mother's arms year after year is a great injustice to her.

Why is it that those who are rich have only the amount of children they need, while the poor have more than they can afford to feed? It all boils down to access, and good access for all.

CHAPTER FOUR

THE MATRIX: THE WOMB OF THE GOSPEL

Meaning of matrix

Noun

1. An environ or material in which something develops; a surrounding medium or structure.
2. From Latin mater "mother" breeding female; matrix "womb"

The Plan of Redemption relies on symbols and codes that are concealed so that the plan may not be counterfeited. During Christ's time here on earth He used parables to reveal truth to the humble seekers and then confuse the ones who love error. When the character of Christ is fully reproduced in us then He will come to take us home with Him.

<u>Kingdom Figures</u>

Wheat	Tares		
1930 – 2016	A.D.	D.T.	K.B.
86 years	30 + 40 + 24		
8 + 6 = 14	94 years		
	9 + 4 = 13		

14	41	Kobe Bryan's age
+14	+41	
28 Hallelujah	82	gnashing of teeth

Dial of Ahaz	
+ 10°	10° +

38	92
John 5 The Pool of Bethesda	Minneapolis – St. Paul
÷2 = 19 baskets of fragments	÷2 = 46 George Floyd's age and last 46 minutes of life

Christ's Number

Mark 15:28 *"And the scripture was fulfilled, which saith, And he was numbered with the transgressors."*

Since Christ was at one point, a part of the prison system. He is well familiar with the operations of it. He was held for 3 days and 3 nights in the heart of the earth He was held prisoner by ungodly men, before He was crucified.

Matthew 12:40 *"For as Jonah was three days and three nights in the belly of a huge whale, so the Son of Man will be three days and three nights in the heart of the earth."*

Thank God, Christ conquered the Prison system and set us free by rising up on the 3rd day.

When Toots Hibbert went to prison centuries later he was given the same number Christ received.

54 - 46

54 (5 + 4) is Jesus' Old Testament number for His name Abaddon. (Revelation 9). This Hebrew name means destroyer.

46 is Christ's New Testament name for His name Apollyon, meaning Exterminator. In the final analysis Christ will exterminate the wicked, root and branch.

Both numbers equal 100 for Psalm 100.

George Floyd's Number

46 + 46 (92)

Kobe Bryan's Number

41 + 24 (65)

Norbert FreeWings

5757 (114)

Queen Olympia

164 + 56 (220)

Trump's Number

CBS - 46 Trump's year of birth
    - 45th Presidency

F	O	X	
6	15	24	= 45

= 9 1 (- 9) June 15, + 4 days to Lazarus' tomb = June 19
  1 9

| Juneteenth 19 19th June | Deliverance from the Anti-Christ |
| 15th June and 4 days to Lazarus' tomb | Trump |

(John 11)

The Virus of Sin

H_1 = 8	Trump total number is '132'

N_1
   = 14
    22
	This is the number of the anti-Christ for this is a number with blood.

+
Covid -19
=   41
   + 91
   132
	In a dream about the paper towel sky turning to blood, we see it's partial fulfillment when Trump went to the island of Puerto Rico and threw paper towels to the victims.

The condition of earth's kingdoms is as fragile as paper towels. Puerto Rico represents the door of judgement.

When Trump mishandled the Corona virus-19 pandemic he added the blood to the paper towel sky with the loss of millions of lives. He fulfilled the dream in every particular as he now must face his own judgement, for he knows he is a mass-killer and a fugitive by the wall of Zion. His losing the presidential score terrifies him for it is his name and number 232. But his score was 232 and not 132.

Well guess who has shown up in this number?

Mr. Toots	54	+	46	=	100
&		132			
Maytals		+ 100			
&					
Christ		232			

This losing presidential score was already predicted in 2018 with the NFL super bowl with the Eagles and the Pats in Minniesota. At one point in the game there was a tie at 32 – 32. The three 3 for Trinity delivers the 232 score. This score is also very disconcerting for Trump because when you subtract 232 from Biden's 306 score/win you get 74 which is Trump's age. That his end has come takes on new meaning!

No wonder Trump has gone to increasing lengths to reverse the score stating that it is rigged. But numbers do not lie do they? So desperate is he, that wants Georgia Raffensperger to change the numbers. If only he could change the setting score he would feel much relieved. But the number is immovable, as the blood on his little hands! It is fixed and now the vanishing hour is here.

"3232"

This Super bowl game tie between the Eagles and the Pats in 2018, reveal a number of things with the number '3'.

1. God came down in the Trinity that day. The Chief Shepherd came to the sheepfold in the form of Quarterback Nick Foles #9 in the "nick" of time.
2. A faithful Ministry has been disclosed to view, to take the field against Satan. He knows that will be his waterloo hence

his supreme effort to eliminate them. He cannot do so, so he brought on covid-19 and the Time of Trouble in the hope of destroying all. This is Satan's third mass-murder attempt: -

i.   Drowning of the Hebrews boys (Exodus 1:22) to kill Moses.
ii. Herod all killing all the infants "from two years" in the hope of doing away with Christ,
iii. Covid-19 to wipe out all the 144,000 living saints and civilization as a whole.

Michael, the great Prince and Deliverer, stood up (Daniel 12:1 and gloriously delivered the saints – all whose names are retained in the Book of Life, (White House Recruiter)

3. The Third Decree

The third decree to rebuild the temple in Ezra's day carried a death sentence. In our day those three decrees are three messages to restore the kingdom, as in the three Angels Messages.

The third decree which is the equivalent to this message of the Judgement of the Living has a death decree in Ezekiel.

God's Vindication

Although Nancy "Anunciata" Pelosi was reluctant to impeach Trump at first, God had decreed for her to make such an announcement that the Hour of Judgement is come. (Revelation). Judgement can no longer be deferred! God Himself was in the proceedings for Schiff was of Adam's line. God has to set things right in the nations and in the church also. here it was seen that the President was impeach! God will vindicate His name by getting rid of all those followers who are not faithful and cause His name to be reproached the heathen. The twin brothers Vindom who helped in the process show that God uses humankind to bring about justice with His help.

Therefore, while He used twin-Vindmans to procure justice in the Great Day of God, He used twin brothers McCourty to announce the Dreadful Day and the gnashing of teeth. Devin McCourty is an American Football who was drafted by the Patriots. He wears #32 jersey and his twin brother is Jason McCourty.

We are called to Court.
Let all the earth keep silence, before Him.

CHAPTER FIVE

THE N.F.L. (NATIONAL FOOTBALL LEAGUE)

The N.F.L. Superbowl game and scores hold a certain fascination for me. I regard myself as the "Official Armchair Quarter." Yeah!

Nissan Stadium – 2019

God used Nissan Stadium in Nashville, Tennessee and the two franchises - Titans vs. Texans to reveal final numbers for the Judgement Day and to close the curtains on the Sanctuary operations as He declared: **It is Done!**

Judgement Scores

December 15, 2019

Texans – 24	Judgement 9 – 5
Titans – 21	Perfection 8 – 6

December 29, 2019

Titans – 35	Finish Line 9 – 7
Houstan – 14	Abandoned in Brandon 10 – 6

The Tennessee Titans who starts out as Texan Oilers represent the Five Wise Virgins with extra oil in their lamps and vessels. The trek to Tennessee was beneficial to them as they advanced to Nissan Stadium where Jehovah-Nissan reside. In the presence of God and the word they grew and prospered. (Matthew 25). The Houstan Texans remained in Texas and they represent the 5-Foolish Virgins who did not take extra-oil with them on the journey homeward. So they ran out of oil and suffered a great loss.

Breakdown of Final Score

Titans	1	2	3	4	T
	7	7	7	14	35

Houston	1	2	3	4	T
	7	0	7	0	14

The Titans had indeed come to perfection as God had shined through them. The wise will shine as the stars in the firmament.

As you'd have noticed, the Texans started out with a perfect score but soon ran out of supply. They recovered through grace and got another perfect score (7). Somehow through carelessness they were on empty again and loss all that they had. Grace had run out. The five foolish virgins had not the connection with Infinite source so they came up with a deficit in the end.

The Word of the Day – Campanology

Noun

the art or practice of bell ringing.

From late the Latin campana "bell"

The Great Day Signal

Isaiah 2:27 "Zion shall be redeemed with judgement, and her converts with righteousness"

    i-   Universe: *cosmos, world, creation*

When Gill Maley made a call regarding my manuscript on December 23, 2019, it signaled the Great Day on the horizon. You see, the 23rd day is the equivalent of the 23rd Psalm about Green Pastures. So why does this date compare to Green Pastures. Gill's work address ends in a zip code '63' which for 6,000 years God has been calling men to the light. For centuries this message has been in the land calling for the a revival and a reformation in the life.

Isaiah 1:4 *"Ah sinful nation, a people laden with iniquity, a seed of evildoers, children that are corruptor: they have forsaken the Lord, they have provoked the Holy One of Isael unto anger, they are gone away backward,"*

This situation will not last much longer and we are called to sound the alarm.

---

marks the 'score' for the five foolish virgins.   63

26

In claiming ⬚ 23 ⬚ more points on the 23rd day she received the Kingdom light and is saved.

Indeed, 2019 was a good year as I received a Mercedes Benz for my 35th wedding anniversary, I saw President Barack Obama in a dream, waiting for the Savior who sky-dived to earth in glory. Robert Smith paid off the student loans of the class of 2019 and their parents' loans as well in an Heave offering at Morehouse. Then Toni-Ann Singh won the Miss World crown for Jamaica, it was a high day and a high year.

The Dreadful Day Signal

Isaiah 3:24 *"And it shall come to pass, that instead of sweet smell there shall be stink; and instead a girdle a rent; and instead of a well set hair baldness; and instead of a stomacher a girding of a sackcloth; and burning instead of beauty."*

The year started out on a dark note with few bright. *Manna: A consecrated GPS Guide to the Promised Land* was released. Then the Covid-19 pandemic raged over the Globe. We witnessed the horrific slayings of George "Perry" Floyd and countless others in racist attacks and the surge in hate crimes and violence.

In the State of the Union Address Rush Limbaugh was awarded the Presidential Medal of Freedom to unleash terror on the world in a Covid-19 attack by President Trump. (Revelation 7).

In these and more signs we knew that the world would never be the same again and a change had to come about, and fast.

On November 20, 2020 I had another terrible dream about the end. This time I was outside my house and when I looked up saw the sky boiling with blood and the cloud black as soot. It was a most terrifying sight to behold when I looked and saw a mangled hand in the fore ground of the sky. It seemed like Bozrah – a kind of slaying and I felt sad as I knew that many Christians were about to perish.

In December I called on Jeremy Carey and Marty Cain to get an update on recent manuscript I had sent on December 23, 2020. This call was not in favor of the lost since Mr. Cain's name means punishment.

Hence those who do not measure us will be destroyed. On December 25, a Nashville bomber destroyed many businesses in the downtown area. He was 63 years old. He planned the attack adjacent to an AT&T network hub.

Handel Re-named Hambel

When we signed up for the internet service, my son Handel was misspelt for Hambel on the Bill. The Ham references the Kingdom of darkness (swine) and the 'bel' for freedom and liberty. The church must be freed from sin and sinners and separated from the guilty in order to 'Rise Up'. God will do a thorough cleansing of His church in the purification soon to take place.

While the sinners in Zion are taken out in destruction, the righteous arise and display their brilliance just as Jupiter and Saturn did in the Great Conjunction of December 21, 2020.

Warnock and the Loud Cry

The call to action or the call to war must be given with certainty. We must give the trumpet a certain sound. Hence Warnock is used by God to declare war on the sins of Babylon. A 'warnock' knock is knocking on the heart's door to leave Babylon because God is about to destroy her with plagues. (Revelation).

Get Out! Leave!

What is an Aphyllos Tree?

Answer: a bare tree.

A time is coming when the earth will tremble like a leaf because of the shaking. Harvest is over.

Carmel Withers

Amos 1:2 "And he said, the Lord will roar from Zion, and utter His voice from Jerusalem, and the habitations of the Shepherds shall mourn and the top of Carmel shall wither."

I Heard the Roar

i – 20

On December 29, I was driving the Benz on i-20 heading home from Ryne Street. As I was about to exit on Wesley Chapel (68) I had to get over to the right lane. It was a really thick traffic so my husband looked out for me to cross over. I was looking with him not realizing I was about to rear end a truck in front of me. We came very close! I heard my husband cry out in a loud voice for me to watch out. Luckily I did not hit the vehicle. God is good. He intends that his voice be now heard in the land as judgement begins at the Seventh-Day Adventist Church. (1 Peter 4:17). Amen.

Yes, God is about to strip the SDA Church bare.

CHAPTER SIX

HAMILTON HOLMES AREA

People must realize by now that these are not ordinary times. Momentous events are ahead of us.

"Fasten Your Seat Belts"

Tuesday, January 5, 2021

I woke up this morning at 5:03 a.m. and the window AC/Heater register 74° Farenheit.

Revelation 7:3 *"Saying, Hurt not the earth, neither the sea, nor the trees, till we have sealed the servants of our God in their foreheads."*

In order for the gospel work to be finished God's sealed people, the 144,000 must be sealed with the seal of the living God to perform their task.

A task to go and rescue God's people out of Babylon. These consecrated workers, 144,000 in number are sufficient to help dispel the darkness and call the people out of a depraved system into the Ark of Safety.

Inspiration declares that if there is any intervening time between the sealing and the slaughter, the winds would blow. Well, we are in the "intervening time" with this next event to come in the slaughter of Ezekiel 9. This will be a literal event!

Dividend Rd: Tile Shop

Dividend Road implies dividing a number by another number. Of the tribe of Simeon and Levi this curse was pronounced:

Genesis 49:7 *"Curse be their anger, for it was fierce; and their wrath for it was cruel; I will divide them in Jacob and scatter them in Israel."*

Dividing, in this case means limiting roles.

Dividend also means 1. A sum of money paid regularly (typically quarterly) by a company to its shareholders out of its profits (or reserves),

When Christ returns He will come with His reward for the saints as the wise virgins enter the Banquet Hall for the Great Supper. Notice that this parable take place in Matthew 25, a quarterly number. We will reap our reward in 2021 for this year fulfils the 25th mark.

Dreams of Reward

In 2020, I dreamed that my sister and I were in a house helping our family friend give birth to three babies in quick succession. After we were through my sister and I went outside and she grabbed my hand and began running towards an open field. We ran and then scaled the wooden fence and landed in a grassy pasture. A caretaker then told us we would soon be given a much larger and better pasture but we were very content.

Another time we were at Kroeger shopping for toiletries. I needed to get up to the loft where they were stored but a woman was up there so I waited. I noticed a lot of soldiers with guns were going up and down the store aisles but they appeared friendly so I conversed with them. The woman in the loft was taking too long to get down so I shouted at her to leave! Then I climbed up the loft and saw that a congregation was seated with their backs to me. I asked someone help to get the paper towels but he wouldn't help me. Then as I waited I turned my head towards the river nearby and saw fireworks going in rapid and splendid succession. It was a most beautiful sight to behold, a grand display of celebration and I woke up.

Another time my husband and I were at a theme park in Sandusky, Ohio. We rode down a roller-coaster so fast that the speed caused heavy sparks of fire on the rails. Wow, it was a very exhilarating ride to the finish, we got to the end of the ride and went to a house nearby.

The work will be cut short in righteousness and this is the very last message of mercy to go forth to a dying world before everything ceases forever!

Dreams Associated with Dividend Road

A man came to my work station and stood by my husband, Norbert, helping him to build display boards. I wanted that area to do my grouting so I asked him to leave. Before he left he took up a few empty boards and lay on them on a trolley and rode outside the door to dispose of them. Those empty boards symbolize the empty vessels of the five-foolish virgins. (Matthew 25).

In another dream that I saw that the tile shop was emptied of all tiles and ceased. All that was left were the four wall and the empty shelves. The floors were filled with dust so workers began sweeping up the dirt. I was glad that a renovation of the shop was about to take place. Soon after that a man took a hose to spray the area and that created a muddy sea. I took a shovel to begin helping to remove the dirt but the gentleman told me to leave it alone which I gladly did. I was happy that the shop was getting a face lift.

Another worker at the shop got a dream as well pertaining to Dividend Road. She saw a dead, white bird on top of a stack of grouted boards. This means life shall be taken from the unfaithful ones in the church, To cement that fact, a friend from Pennsylvania came and worked for a short time with us. She helped to clean up the lunch room and bathrooms. Before she left she purchased a vase with beautiful, artificial flowers in it and placed it atop the snack dispenser in the kitchen. The "dead white bird" got her cemetery flowers after all.

The temple will be cleansed of all defilement and sin.

Some Workers who Helped to Announce the Nearness of the Time

Hopeton "Rooster" Williams came on the scene to announce 'daybreak' and that the season of cockcrowing is over. (Mark 13:35). This word occurs only in Mark 13:35 where it is evidently used to designate the third of four parts into which the night was divided – 'at even, or at midnight, or at the cockcrowing or in the morning.'

After several months at work Hopeton left, and his wife, June, too in 2019 and never returned,

Denzil from Anguilla island then showed up to work as a grouter. This man from the "snake island" (Anguilla – the eel) portends for those who do not have the seal of God for they will be cut off from the true congregation. He represents those who will gnash their teeth in anguish at being locked outside the Marriage supper. (Matthew 13, 25).

In recent times, Anthony, another grouter joined us with a healing name – surgeon. Some will experience the fulfilment of their desires and will be made whole. Other will not recover from their terminal diagnosis.

The Culling in the Church

My sister, who resides in Canada, recently moved from her Martha Eaton address to a Culford address. She is my mother's third child and is used to depict the "culling" in God flock at this time.

Another star who drives home this fact is Kimberly McCullough who was born in Bell Flower, California. She is an American actress best known for her role as Robin Scorpio on the soap opera General Hospital.

Yes, the Master Surgeon and Healer is here. The alarm has gone off for salutation has come to the children of men. The Great Physician now is here to bind up all Covid-19 wounds. He will separate in death though, those with the incurable Covid-18 - a terminal disease called selfishness. It takes the lives of all those who do not get the victory over the "world, the flesh and the devil."

Sin Finally Put in its Place

> Poner – (to put)
> Pretrite tense

My Spanish Lecturer always related to us how her male students at school loved the Spanish conjugation of the verb PONER to put since it was a corruption of her name "heron".

Yo - puse	nos - pusimas
Tu - pusiste	vos – pusteis
El, ella - puso	ellos – pusieron

The plural form they always would always pronounce as "pussy-heron" inserting an 'h' where none was needed.

In the end, the big cat catches the mouse. The trap used is always a "Hunter Rat-trap.

Kemp Governor – the Porter

Governor Kemp's middle name is Porter. None will be given admittance through the door who is not worthy. Those without the wedding garment on will be escorted out.

Trump cannot get the Georgia vote to change even though he tried numerous desperate effort to do so. He has been weigh in the balances and found wanting. He will now be subjected to the full force of the justice he deserves. Number never lie!

Sarah the Freewoman, Hagar the Bondwoman, the Digital Divide

In 2014 while I worked at Rick Victors home in Georgia I changed my Judie646 Yahoo account to wjudy127@gmail.com.

I never realized until recently that that change represented one of transformation. You see, Sarah died at age 127 and that 27 in fullness represents a spiritual rebirth (2nd birth)

$$9 \times 3 = 27$$

Genesis 23:1 *"And Sarah was a hundred and seven and twenty years old: these were the years of the life of Sarah."*

So my email represented the first fruit unto God. (Revelation 14)

1. wjudy127@gmail.com
   If my email represented the first fruits, then Regina King of 227 fame must represent the second fruit.

2. Kregina227@gmail.com
   That light will fill the earth with glory. God used the hydro-electricity from the Hoover Dam to explain it.

3. Hherbert727@gmail.com
   Hoover Dam is 727 feet high. That segment in the church who are a part of Hagar's house of bondage are represented by a '427' phone number,

4. T.D427@gmail.com
   Those on the fence who refuse to make a clear decision in favor of the cross are represented by August Wilson of 'fences'. He lived above a grocery store on 1727 Bedford Ave, Pittsburg, P.A.

5. KAugust1727@gmail.com
   The address of the work site at Dividend Road is 5327.

6. Sq.Snapfinger5327@gmail.com
   We have all information at our finger tips. In his book Abandoned in Brandon on page 127 Alonzo declares that we must not be afraid of failure:

   "Moses failed, Peter failed, Abraham failed, Jacob failed, Isaac failed and David failed, yet they were all successful giants for God and humanity."

   The only failure here is Alonzo S who failed to heed the instructions in Micah 6:9 to hear ye the rod… Of such the very next page in his book is a blank page serving as a reminder that he is blotted out of the Book ok Life.

7. SAlonzo0027@gmail.com
    Spued out. (Revelation 3).

    Whereas page is blank in his book, <u>Abandoned in Brandon</u> our
    book <u>Manna: A Consecrated GPS Guide into the Promised</u>
    <u>Land</u> has this great verse on page 128:

    Exodus 3:14 *"And God said to Moses, I AM THAT I AM: and*
    he said, thus shalt thou say unto the children of Israel, I AM hath
    sent me unto you."

Here then is the church triumphant.

8. The Victory Church127@Mt Zion's Land

The 34th President – Dwight David Eisenhower

This president represents the perfection of truth – the 3-fold truth and
the 4-fold truth. The name Eisenhower means "hewer of iron" the iron
that represent Rome. It was during Eisenhower tenure that we got to
see the ugly face of Rome. In 1955, the 14-year old Emmet Till went to
Money, Mississippi and was brutally murdered. Barbed wire was used
to fasten the body in the Tallahatchie River where his body was thrown.
In 2020 we witness a resurgence of Rome in the killing death of George
Floyd by the hand of Derick Chauvin. It interesting to note that he was
born on the same birthday as George Floyd on October 14.

"Ike" as the president was called is a name that means "Laughter". The
scoffers in Noah's time mocked and laughed at the thought of rain. So,
many nowadays laugh at the idea of God setting up a kingdom-church
here in a sinful world. Yet it is bound to happen.

You see the fullness of time has come. At the first presidential debate
between Biden and Trump, Biden had to warn Trump to be quiet as
God was in the arena and he needed to "shut up." The emissaries of

heaven came for Trump and told him it's over. Trump was taken to the Walter Reed in Bethesda on the pretext of Covid-19 infection. He had to leave the White House as a command was issued and was to be read on October 13. Yet he left before for he was to go there for an exchange. He was to take on the condition of the man at the pool of Bethesda, (John 5) and became a cripple. His four-day stay labeled him anti-Christ, the "colon man,"

For us, it marked the fulfillment our dreams. We had made it to the Finish Line. Just as the paralytic waited 38 years before Jesus showed up, just so humanity has waited 38 years for Jesus to show up in Bethesda inside 2020. I know He was at the pool, for I saw Jesus descend headways to earth on November 20, 2019 in a dream.

Rivers of Life

The Platte River in Nebraska (310 miles), represent the crown of thorns plaited for Christ's head. The Crown of thorns will become a crown of glory.

The Wabash shining river in Indiana is 503 miles long. The source at Fort Recovery remind us we will recover it all! Wabash a type of the Bashan spiritual pasture.

Rivers of Death

The Snake River in the U.S. is the largest North American at 1,078 miles. This river runs through Idaho.

The Rio Minho in Jamaica is the longest in the country. (57.7 miles) 92.8 kilometer. The river originate in Dry Harbour mountains which forms part of the Cockpit country in Jamaica. It's mouth ends in Portland Point in Clarendon. Min.HO is really a red river.

The Milk River in May Pen is an witness that sin will finally run its course.

Hamilton Holmes Area, Atlanta

We are now on Ryne Street and Hood Avenue. We renovate a house on 1725 Ryne Street for friend Walter Stith.

Ryne Street: name means "Little King"

The king has returned to rule. We walk on streets of gold henceforth.

Hood Avenue: short for Royal Priesthood. We are on Glory avenue. A Royal Priesthood, a holy nation. (1Peter 2:9)

Walter Stith

The 'alter' in Walter's means that the Saviour has suddenly come to his temple. (Malchiah 3 & 4).

The name 'Stith' means cattleman.

We are now in the vineyard.

The Shittim wood, Exodus 35, is now transformed into Stith – no more dung.

Tabernacle

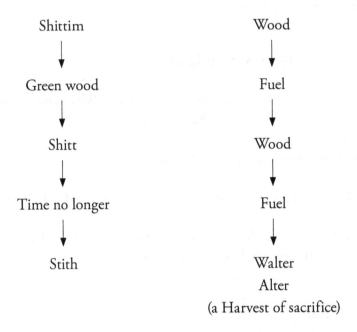

Shittim → Green wood → Shitt → Time no longer → Stith

Wood → Fuel → Wood → Fuel → Walter

Alter

(a Harvest of sacrifice)

Sin cut off. Cut tile Montalcino number │ 92 │ cut asunder.

Hood Avenue: Priesthood

Neighbourhood

Sin cut off – The great Castration
Marriage supper - the Great Erection
Ryne Street - King's Highway Royalty comes to town
Jon Ossoff represents the Bossom of Father Abraham.
Loeffler represent the spoon

[Measuring]   [Silver]

Holy Spirit and Squirrels

The Holy Spirit encourages us to store up the truth as do squirrels who store up for the winter. The word **'ir'**, Spanish for to go is in the middle of the names. It is the Holy Spirit who brings us light and truth in the form of messages that guide us forward.

The Houston Texan remained behind in Texas and represents the 5-foolish virgins. As you see in the second score sheet they ran out of oil in the second and fourth play.

The 5-wise virgins made a display in the Great Conjunction one year later (12.21.20) in Jupiter and Saturn. The fate of the 5-foolish virgins was seen in the bomb blast at AT&T in Nashville (12.25.20), so the wise virgins get to consummate the marriage on Hood Avenue.

The Dividends pour out at the quarter, 1725 Ryne Street. The 5-foolish virgins felt the knife of castration as they lost on the kingdom. The transformation of life is very important to cross the Digital divide. Two relatives who became presidents tell by their lives and death how important it is to get the transforming power of God that I label 10^0 on the dial of Ahaz. You want to get eternal life you have to get your 10^0.

Teddy Roosevelt and FDR were fifth cousins. FDR was the 32nd president of the USA and his initials are 28 points. He lived a life of pleasing the flesh. He was a paralytic from polio disease.

TR is one of the four faces on Mt. Rushmore in Dakota. His face immortalized thus and serves to remind us that right-doing (righteousness) promotes a man. The four figures on the Mount reminds us of the Rock who guides us and the Spirit of truth who will outpour power and glory on us in the carrying out of the last message of hope to earth's inhabitants.

He died in warm springs Ga – landing in "Hot water" and was buried in Hyde Park to be hidden away in the earth. Teddy Roosevelt was a righteous was man who served God and then went on to become the 20th president of the US. His initial equal 38 points – 10⁰ more than FDR. This president died at Oyster Bay and rest now at Young Memorial Cemetery – a sign of youthful restoration.

Sing Sing Correctional Facility

Hunter "burisma" the head of the serpent and sets the prisoner free. (Genesis 3:15)

Address
354 Hunter St. Ossining
NY 10562

President Barack Obama fulfills Isaiah 52 with his book "A Promised Land." He then follows up with … "Of Thee I Sing" a letter to his daughters.

Isaiah 52:1 *"Awake, awake put on thy strength, O Zion: put on thy beautiful garments, O Jerusalem, the holy city: for henceforth there shall no more come into thee the uncircumcised and the uncleaned."*

vs. 2 *"Shake thyself from the dust; arise, and sit down, O Jerusalem: loose thyself from the band of thy neck, O captive daughter of Zion."*

vs. 9 *"Break forth into joy, sing together, ye waste places of Jerusalem: for the Lord hath comforted his people, he hath redeemed Jerusalem,"*

Numbers 21:17 *"Then Israel sang this song, Spring up, O well: sing ye unto it:"*

March 15, 2021

In High School I studied *Great Expectations* by Dickens as my Literature text. This book forecast the Great Day of God. We also studied Julius Caesar, the great Roman statesman. A soothsayer predicted his death on March 15, the ides of March, and that was exactly what happened as his friend [Brutus] killed him to save the republic. Now I'd like to have this 8th volume to be released on Monday, March 15, 2021 on the ides of March.

Word of the Day: Wot

Wot – to know

Numbers 22:6 *"Come now therefore, I pray thee, curse me this people; for they are too mighty for me: peradventure I shall prevail...for I wot not that he whom thou blesses is bless, and whom thou cursest is cursed."*

God to Baalam

vs.12 *"Thou shalt not go with them, thou shalt, thou shalt not curse the people for they are blessed."*

CHAPTER SEVEN

IT'S CRUNCH TIME

It's the end of harvest for the church, hence His grace runs out on the people as the oil run out of their vessels. God's grace. God removed Ruth Bader Gingsburg from service to denote the time for rebirth is over.

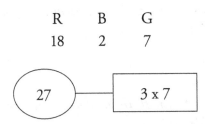

He replaced her with a name that is associated with rocks for the coneys are feeble, yet they build their homes in rocks. (Proverbs 30:26)

Revelations 6:16 *"And so to the mountains and rocks, fall on us, and hide us from the face of him that sitteth on the throne, and from the wrath of the lamb:"*

We are in the Judgement Hour at the Bar of God.

[Amy Coney Barret]

Thomas J. Vilsack, Secretary of Agriculture has a sack in which is Joseph's golden cup, (Genesis 4:4)

Not golden cup – a silver cup that reminds us of our silver lining. Yes, after the long night of sin and decay, God grants us the silver lining of a New Day! Yes, the filthy cups at Cup Foods, filled with all forms of abominations will be broken and cast away. At least Chauvin is to be judge and charged. The cup of trembling must be removed. Amen.

Ms. Fudge who replaces Ben Solomon Carson as Secretary of HUD (Housing and Urban Development) reminds us of those who get inside the house by "fudging" their rèsumè like Ben Carson, will be cast out! See how quickly the tables have turned on him. On the SDA current logo, he represents the first caterpillar sign with 18 legs. The other caterpillar sign belongs to Alonzo Smith who spent 18 days in the hospital due to Covid-19 infection. Both of the order of Mahershalalhasbaz – born only once after the flesh. (Isaiah 7, 8).

Senator Kelly Loeffler named 'Loeffler' means "spoon maker". From that we get the "measuring spoon" and the "silver spoon."

Jon Ossoff and Stacy Abrams are symbols of Father Abraham in whose bosom we rest. Ossoff – bosom of Father Abraham

Stacy Abrams means 'fruitful one.'

Ms. Yellen –Janet, an American economist handles the money. She represents the 'Yellen' of the Loud Cry Movement.

"Come out of her my people!" (Revelation 18)

Sis. E.G. White Impressive Dream

While at Battle Creek in August 1868, she dreamed of being in a large body of people. They were prepared to journey. As they progressed the path grew narrower until they had to abandon their belongings and horses and go on bare feet. Down below the abyss she heard the sounds of mirth and revelry. They heard the profane oath, the vulgar jest and low vile songs. They heard the war songs and the dance songs. They heard instrumental music and loud laughter mingled with cursing and cries of anguish and bitter wailing.

A cord was let down from heaven to assist the faithful travelers. Before them finally, on the other side of a chasm was a beautiful field of green grass, about six inches high. They swung themselves into the beautiful field beyond. Voices were heard in triumphant praise to God. (2 Shepherd Rod page 594 – 7).

This crisis that we faced has brought us to Green Pasture where we must now lay down. (Psalm 23)

That the kingdom is here and now is crystal clear for why do we have to keep our 6 feet apart? If yours is longer than mine, please report to me.

Our Sienna van, the one that is our work van, is wobbly at the wheels. She is shaking like "Sloopy in Ohio" for the Master is here, And why do you think that the Greek storms in December began to speak in tongues? They recognize the Master of oceans, earth and sky is here. Have you recognized him as yet?

Word of the Day – Trouville

Noun:

1. A lucky find
    We have been forgiven of all our sins and now God bestows His favor on us by restoring to us the kingdom – church.

Word of the Day – Roister

1. Enjoy oneself or celebrate in a noisy or boisterous way.

God will then fill our mouths with laughter like President "Ike".

Psalm 126:2 *"Then our mouth filled with laughter, and our tongue with singing: then said they among the heathen, The Lord hath done great things for them."*

The Great Conjunction on December 21, 2020 reflects the joining of the fourth angel with the third angel message to create a Loud Cry.

Jupiter – the star of Jupiter means shining one or blazing star. Jupiter was the god of thunder, lightning and storms. We experience the following Greek storms in 2020:

Delta   Zeta [for Cathenne, Zeta Jones]
Eta
Epsilon   Iota

Saturn is the god of Agriculture. We are reminded of the sickle and the Atlanta Falcons whose name means "sickle".

Time to Reap!

When Trump held up the Bible at St. John's Episcopal Church in June (2020) in silence it spoke volumes that the end is here. The Book is closed and judgement now ensues. The Bible that condemned him renders him speechless and he hold us a death certificate in reality instead.

Today, January 6, 2021

With Raphael Warnock and Jon Ossoff winning both senate seats in Georgia, it marks a new beginning. The defeat of David Perdue and Kelly Loeffler signifies that our dominion has been restored. What a victory! The enemy has had our birth certificate, our birthright – papers and our land title in his back pocket for a long time. He put our birth certificate in his pocket and told us we descended from monkeys and apes! He held on our land title and told us we must live in ghettos and projects because the mansions Christ has gone to prepare for us is "fake news." That is why HUD Secretary Ben Carson choose the Housing the Real Estate Mogul offered as a great deal! (John 14).

The enemy folded our birthright papers in his pocket and treated us as "disposables" instead of "lively stones" and a Royal Priesthood. (1 Peter 2)

Why do you think that Chauvin had his hand in his pocket as he snuffed out the life of George Floyd by kneeling in his neck?

There is another pocket issue also, for when President John Trump returned from Walter Reed Hospital after covid-19 treatment, the first thing he did once he got to the White House was to take off his mask and put it in his *empty pocket*. Hallelujah! He no longer has any dominion over us as we are free. He has been unmasked by the Great Jehovah and broken without hand. His water-loo starts now.

All the barriers and stumbling blocks he has erected in our path have been blown away. It's a glorious day. We possess our possession! We are a holy priesthood. (1 Peter 2). Amen.

CONCLUSION

How Great Thou Art

O Lord my God, when I in awesome
wonder
Consider all the world Thy hands have
made
I see the stars, I hear the rolling
thunder
Thy power throughout the Universe
Displayed

[Refrain]
Then sings my soul, my Savior God
to Thee
How great Thou art, how great
Thou art
Then sings my soul, my Savior
God to Thee
How great Thou art, how great Thou
Art

[verse 2]
When through the woods, and forest
glades I wander

And hear the birds sing sweetly
in the trees
When I look down, from lofty
mountain grandeur
And see the brook, and feel the
gentle breeze

[verse 3]
And when I thing that God, His Son
not sparing
Sent Him to die, I scarce can take
it in
That on the cross, my burden gladly
bearing
He bled and died to take away
my sin

[verse 4]
When Christ shall come, with shouts
of acclamation
And take me home, what joy shall
fill my heart
Then I shall bow, in humble adoration
And then proclaim: "My God, how great
Thou art!"

Visit us at One Word Advent Ministry.net
Address: 2500 Mt Carmel Drive
River Road Decatur, GA 30034

Printed in the United States
by Baker & Taylor Publisher Services